The Greatest Show on Earth: The History of the Ringling Bros. and Barnum & Bailey Circus

By Charles River Editors

Early 20th century advertisement of the Barnum and Bailey Circus.

About Charles River Editors

Charles River Editors provides superior editing and original writing services across the digital publishing industry, with the expertise to create digital content for publishers across a vast range of subject matter. In addition to providing original digital content for third party publishers, we also republish civilization's greatest literary works, bringing them to new generations of readers via ebooks.

Sign up here to receive updates about free books as we publish them, and visit Our Kindle Author Page to browse today's free promotions and our most recently published Kindle titles.

Introduction

Ringling Bros. and Barnum & Bailey Circus

"I was a farmhand, a merchant, a clerk, a boss, a theater director and a bank director; I lived in prisons and palaces, I knew poverty and abundance, I've traveled extensively on two continents, I've met all kinds of people and seen the human character in all its guises, and time and again I have been in the greatest danger. Amidst such a diversity of events, I had to undergo difficult times, but I'm definitely not complaining, and I believe that my life was a happy one, because I always saw the positive side of things." – P.T. Barnum

Americans have loved traveling circuses for generations, and none represent the country's love for entertainment quite like the most famous of them all, the Ringling Bros. and Barnum & Bailey Circus. The five brothers who started a circus in Wisconsin, as well as P.T. Barnum, have had their names become synonymous with the circus, so it's only fitting that the manner in which these men entered the business and the merging of their traveling circuses together also make for great stories.

Circus promoters have long been viewed as somewhat shady hucksters, but none could top P.T. Barnum, who used a blend of traditional circus entertainment, freak show exhibits, and outright hoaxes to create "The Greatest Show on Earth". Barnum introduced America to Jumbo the Elephant, one of the most legendary acts in the history of the circus, as well as "exhibits" like Joice Heth, an elderly African American woman Barnum advertised as a 161 year old who nursed George Washington. He also notoriously perpetrated hoaxes with General Tom Thumb and claimed to have a live mermaid, so it's no surprise that Barnum is often apocryphally quoted as saying, "There's a sucker born every minute." While he didn't actually say that, he said something similar: "Nobody ever lost a dollar by underestimating the taste of the American public."

Around the same time that Barnum was operating the Barnum & Bailey's circus, the Ringling Brothers were engaging in more traditional circus activities in Wisconsin. As their traveling circus became better known in the late 1880s, it was advertised as the "Ringling Brothers United Monster Shows, Great Double Circus, Royal European Menagerie, Museum, Caravan, and Congress of Trained Animals". The Ringling Brothers were eventually successful enough that they were able to buy Barnum's circus after Barnum had already died, and they merged the traveling circuses together in 1919.

The Greatest Show on Earth: The History of the Ringling Bros. and Barnum & Bailey Circus examines the origins of the famous circuses, the background of the important individuals involved, and their merger into the most famous circus of all. Along with pictures of important people, places, and events, you will learn about "The Greatest Show on Earth" like never before, in no time at all.

The Greatest Show on Earth: The History of the Ringling Bros. and Barnum & Bailey Circus

Chapter 1: Joice Heth

"My first appearance upon this stage was on the 5th day of July, Anno Domini 1810. Independence Day had gone by, the cannons had ceased to thunder forth their remembrances of our National Anniversary, the smoke had all cleared away, the drums had finished their rattle, and when peace and quiet were restored, I made my debut. This propensity of keeping out of harm's way had always stuck by me." – P.T. Barnum

Phineas Taylor Barnum was born on July 5, 1810, just missing Independence Day by a few hours. The timing couldn't have been better, because the boy born that day was destined to become an all-American symbol of ingenuity and cunning, not to mention the epitome of self-promoting advertisement. His father, Philo Barnum, was an innkeeper in their home town of Bethel, Connecticut whose family had come to the United States more than 100 years earlier, as part of the first wave of settlers after Jamestown and Plymouth. Phineas' mother, Irene, had been born a Taylor and was the daughter of a well-known politician and schemer, Phineas Taylor, after whom she named her son. Barnum grew up in awe of his cunning grandfather, who favored him over his younger siblings: "My grandfather was decidedly a wag. He was a practical joker. He would go farther, wait longer, work harder and contrive deeper to carry out a practical joke, than for anything else under heaven." In many ways, Phineas Taylor established the template that P.T. Barnum would use to make his mark in the world.

As a child, Barnum excelled in arithmetic but was too lazy to do any real physical labor, much to his father's dismay. He made his first trip to New York when he was 12, working as the hireling of a man driving a herd of cattle to the city to sell. Like most children in town, he attended Sunday School each Sunday, and each week, a quiz was given that, if passed, would earn the scholar a small reward. Barnum's answer to one of these quizzes was preserved, and it provides a sense of his understanding of human nature. The question was from the Biblical story of Mary and Martha: "But one thing is needful and Mary hath chosen the good part, which shall not be taken away from her. What is the one thing needful?" Barnum replied:

"This question, 'What is the one thing needful?' is capable of receiving various answers, depending much upon the persons to whom it is addressed. The merchant might answer that the one thing needful is plenty of customers to buy liberally without beating down, and to pay cash for all their purchases. The farmer might reply that the one thing needful is large harvests and high prices. The physician might answer that it is plenty of patients. The lawyer might be of opinion that it is an unruly community always engaged in bickerings and litigations. The clergyman might reply, 'It is a fat salary, with multitudes of sinners seeking salvation and paying large pew rents.' The sensible bachelor might exclaim, 'It is a pretty wife, who loves her husband, and who knows how to sew on buttons.' The maiden might answer, 'It is a good husband who will love, cherish, and protect me while life shall last.' But the proper answer and, doubtless, that which applied to the case of Mary, would be, 'The one thing needful is to believe in the Lord Jesus Christ, follow in His footsteps, love God, and obey His commandments, love our fellow-men, and embrace every opportunity of administering to their necessities.' In short, the one thing needful is to live a life that we can always look back upon with satisfaction and be enabled ever to contemplate its termination with trust in Him who has so kindly vouchsafed it to us, surrounded us with innumerable blessings if we have but the heart and the wisdom to receive them in a proper manner."

Barnum finally found his niche in life as a store keeper, for while he had no use for stocking shelves or keeping books, he did love haggling over prices and convincing people to buy things that they didn't need with money that they didn't have. He also worked with America's first lottery in the late 1820s. Around this time, he met and fell in love with Charity Hallett, and the two soon married. Barnum would later observe, "I was at that time little more than nineteen years of age. I have long felt assured, that had I waited twenty years longer, I could not have found another woman so well suited to my disposition and so valuable as a wife, a mother, and a friend; yet I do not approve of nor recommend too early marriages. Young persons' minds should become more matured before they venture to decide upon the most important event which can occur to them in a lifetime. Marriage has been called 'a lottery,' 'taking a leap in the dark,' etc. It is, to say the least, a serious ordinance, deserving serious thought. Hasty marriage, and especially the marriage of boys and girls, has, in my opinion, been the cause of untold misery in thousands of instances…"

The young couple would go on to enjoy a happy life together, but Charity was always the shyer, more nervous one, and she rightly wondered which of her husband's next schemes would send her to a new mansion or the Poor House. Their first child, daughter Caroline, was born a few years later on May 27, 1833.

Naturally, Barnum soon grew bored of running his store. He needed something more interesting to do, so he decided to open an auction house, specializing in used books. In early 19th century New England, this was a lucrative trade, as reading and thrift were both highly prized. Barnum also made money speculating on real estate, using his unique knowledge of the area to buy low and sell high.

While working for the first state lottery in Connecticut, he became interested in politics and, with his grandfather's support, secured a local office. However, he angered members of the staid Calvinist church, descendants of the even stricter Puritans, by fighting their famous "blue laws", which prohibited everything from dancing to celebrating Christmas. What really bothered him, however, was their stand against his money-making lottery. In 1829, Barnum founded *The Herald of Freedom*, a political newspaper, in his new home in Danbury, Connecticut. He used the paper primarily as a vehicle to castigate churchmen who opposed his plans, and the churchmen responded with less than perfect Christian charity by filing lawsuits against him for libel. They also had him prosecuted on similar charges, and he was convicted and spent two months in the local prison. These woes in his early life only solidified his beliefs, and he left his incarceration more dedicated than ever to promoting the liberal agenda in Connecticut.

When Barnum finally lost his battle against the Calvinists and the lottery was banned in Connecticut in 1834, he decided to move to a more urban and, he hoped, progressive area. He sold his small shop in Danbury and moved his family to New York City. It was there that he discovered his true calling in showmanship, though he would later observe, "I can say that the least deserving of all my efforts in the show line was the one which introduced me to the business, a scheme in no sense of my own devising, one which had been for some time before the public, and which had so many vouchers for its genuineness that at the time of taking possession of it I honestly believed it to be genuine." In 1835, he bought a very elderly African-American woman, Joice Heth, and claimed she was George Washington's nurse when he was a child. At his coaching, the woman, frail and blind though she was, would speak briefly to small groups about her life caring for the infant future president. According to the advertisement for her show, "Joice Heth is unquestionably the most astonishing and interesting curiosity in the World! She was the slave of Augustine Washington, (the father Gen. Washington) and was the first person who put clothes on the unconscious infant, who, in after days, led our heroic fathers on to glory, to victory, and freedom. To use her own language when speaking of the illustrious Father of this Country, 'she raised him'. Joice Heth was born in the year 1674, and has, consequently, now arrived at the astonishing age of 161 years."

Despite the incredible claim about her age, people still flocked to pay a few cents to meet her. In fact, Barnum would later claim that he made $1,500 a week during their 7 month long show. At the same time, since there were plenty who doubted Barnum's claim, he decided to use their doubt to his advantage. He promised the public that, upon the woman's death, her body would be publically autopsied, a humiliation and desecration that was abhorrent to the more sensitive folks of the era but intriguing to Barnum's primary audience. Thus, when Heth finally passed away in February 1836, Barnum scheduled the promised autopsy and charged 1,500 people 50 cents each to witness it. He hired a respected surgeon, Dr. David L. Rogers, to perform the procedure in the large New York City Saloon, and when Rogers declared publicly that the body he was examining could not be more than 80 years old at the time of her death, Barnum took the news in stride by announcing to his audience that it was not Heth's body but another elderly woman. He claimed that Heth, now going on 162 years old, was actually touring Europe. It was only years later that Barnum would admit that the entire thing was a hoax.

Chapter 2: The Barnum American Museum

"The show business has all phases and grades of dignity, from the exhibition of a monkey to the exposition of that highest art in music or the drama which secures for the gifted artists a world-wide fame Princes well might envy. Men, women, and children who cannot live on gravity alone need something to satisfy their gayer, lighter moods and hours, and he who ministers to this want is, in my opinion, in a business established by the Creator of our nature. If he worthily fulfills his mission and amuses without corrupting, he need never feel that he has lived in vain." – P.T. Barnum

At the time of Heth's death, Barnum was touring the country with "Barnum's Grand Scientific and Musical Theater." He was enjoying reasonable success with this project until the Panic of 1837 hit. This economic depression was similar to the Great Depression that would hit the country a century later, and it resulted in people having little money to spend on things like entertainment and traveling shows. For the next three years, Barnum would get by any way he could, supporting his family (which now included a second daughter, Helen, born in April 1840) with odd jobs and short performances until 1841, when he bought Scudder's American Museum.

Located at a prime location on the corner of Broadway and Ann Street in New York City, Scudder's was a huge five story home of unusual sights from around the world. Barnum wasted no time renaming the edifice the Barnum American Museum and threw all his time, energy and money into recreating the place in his own image. He painted the exterior walls bright, gaudy colors, complete with large murals of animals and interesting natural scenes. He hung brightly colored flags and banners in front to attract attention and lit the place up at night so it could be seen up and down Broadway. The use of limelight on the building was itself an attraction, as the method for providing bright light to draw attention to places had only recently been perfected. Barnum also had a garden planted on the flat roof, offered balloon rides over New York City every day, and hired musicians to offer free entertainment to people who wished to stop and enjoy a little music in front of his new business. True to form, Barnum made sure that he hired the worst performers possible, in the hopes that the terrible music outside would compel people to quickly enter the building to get away from it.

The Barnum American Museum

When Barnum opened his museum to the public on New Year's Day 1842, he claimed that he wanted it to be a place where families could come together to enjoy an entertaining and educational experience. However, what he really wanted to do was turn a profit. As a result, the museum soon became a strange mix of lecture hall, zoo, theater and freak show, and in a way that far exceeded even Barnum's wildest dreams, it became the very center of 19th century American popular culture. Before long, no trip to the big city was complete without a visit to the Barnum American Museum, where people could see the latest oddities from around the world, or so it was advertised. An estimated 38 million people visited the museum from 1841-1865, a number that was higher than the nation's entire population in 1860.

To be fair, the museum was not just a collection of strange items, because it did serve an educational purpose also. At a time when most people rarely traveled more than a hundred miles from the place where they were born, Barnum American Museum allowed young and old to see things and experience aspects of life that they could enjoy nowhere else. School children were encouraged to visit the caged animals and see different types of life, while the large aquarium allowed them to get close to animals from the seas, including a white whale. While these animals would be considered badly mistreated by today's standards, they were properly cared for by the standards of knowledge of the day.

Then there were the paintings and the wax museum, which were often designed to recreate events from American and world history. There were even live performances of plays in the "Lecture Room" and theater. One night, there might be a troupe of actors performing one of Shakespeare's plays, while the next day might have a dour woman giving a lecture on the temperance movement. If people wanted it and would pay to see it, Barnum would happily provide it.

Barnum soon filled his museum with everything from the sublime to the ridiculous. He displayed unique tools used by cutting edge scientists of the day, as well as a flea circus. He had the trunk from a tree that had supposedly once shaded Jesus and his disciples in one room, and a dog supposedly working a weaving loom in the other. Larger rooms featured an oyster bar cut from the Chesapeake coast and a rifle range.

The elegant lecture room, described by one publication as "one of the most elegant and recherché halls of its class to be found anywhere", offered "every species of entertainment…from grave to gay, from lively to severe" and was "judiciously purged of every semblance of immorality." Barnum brought in glass blowers and taxidermists to demonstrate their crafts, and he held pretty-baby contests that drew in proud parents from all over the city. He hosted a trained seal named Ned and trained bears taught by a man named Grizzly Adams. The lecture room also featured vaudeville performances, with musicians, ventriloquists and minstrels in blackface. Eventually the museum would be open 15 hours a day, 6 days a week, and when Barnum noticed that more paying customers could not get in because the halls were becoming too crowded, he famously hung signs directing people, "This Way to the Egress". The public, anxious to see this "egress", passed excitedly through the door and outside before they realized that "egress" was another word for exit.

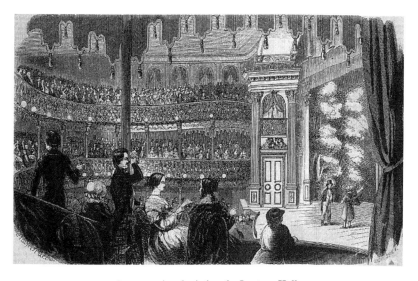

An engraving depicting the Lecture Hall.

One of the things that made Barnum's museum so popular was that he was more than happy to invent items with which to fascinate the public, even if no such item actually existed. His first example of this was the now famous "Fiji mermaid." Barnum rented this oddity from a Boston rival, Moses Kimball, in 1842, but while the creature floating in the jar of formaldehyde was described as a mermaid, it was actually the body of a very young monkey with a fish tail sewn on over its legs. Barnum leased the item long term for $12.50 per week and then marketed it as having been caught by his friend Dr. J. Griffin, a pseudonym for Barnum's business associate Levi Lyman. For his part, Barnum saw nothing wrong with what he was doing, justifying the hoaxes by saying they were just "advertisements to draw attention...to the Museum." He added, "I don't believe in duping the public, but I believe in first attracting and then pleasing them."

A newspaper's depiction of Barnum's "Fiji mermaid" in 1842.

One of the museum's most famous "exhibits" was "General Tom Thumb", who was advertised as "The Smallest Person That Ever Walked Alone." This time there was less deception involved, because Charles Stratton, who played Thumb, really was a dwarf and was actually a distant cousin of Barnum's. When Barnum heard through the family grapevine that he had relatives with a child who had stopped growing at six months of age, he was fascinated and contacted them. He offered them a significant sum of money if they would let their son, then 4 years old, come work for him. The elder Stratton struck a deal with Barnum, and the two remained in business until the former's death in 1855.

Under Barnum's tutelage, the young boy learned to sing, dance and do impersonations. Though he was only 4 years old when he first appeared at the museum in 1842, he was a precocious child who made Barnum's claims that he was actually 11 seem plausible. He toured the country the following year as part of an act developed for him by Barnum, which featured him singing and dancing, as well as doing impersonations of famous people of the time, like

Napoleon Bonaparte. People flocked to see him, making the show a huge success.

General Tom Thumb in 1848.

General Tom Thumb in 1861.

Building on his spreading fame in America, Barnum took Stratton on a tour through Europe, where he appeared in many important royal courts. While in London, he was presented to Queen Victoria and her court. Barnum would later describe the scene:

> "We were conducted through a long corridor to a broad flight of marble steps, which led to the Queen's magnificent picture gallery, where her Majesty and Prince Albert, the Duchess of Kent, and twenty or thirty of the nobility were awaiting our arrival. They were standing at the further end of the room when the doors were thrown open, and the General walked in looking like a wax doll gifted with the power of locomotion. Surprise and pleasure were depicted on the

countenances of the royal circle on beholding this remarkable specimen of humanity so much smaller than they had evidently expected to find him. The General advanced with a firm step, and as he came within hailing distance made a very graceful bow and exclaimed, 'Good evening, ladies and gentlemen.' A burst of laughter followed this salutation. The Queen then took him by the hand, led him about the gallery, and asked him many questions, the answers to which kept the party in an uninterrupted strain of merriment. The General familiarly informed the Queen that her pictures were 'first-rate,' and told her he should like to see the Prince of Wales. The Queen replied that the Prince had retired to rest, but that he should see him on some future occasion. The General then gave his songs, dances, and imitations, and after a conversation with Prince Albert and all present, which continued for more than an hour, we were permitted to depart."

Of course, had the Queen known that the "man" whom she had granted an audience to was actually only six years old, she certainly would not have been amused. She would have been even more shocked to learn that when he was back in America the following year, the boy began smoking cigars and drinking wine with those attending his performances.

Regardless, the European tour was a huge success and was extended into Russia, where Stratton was entertained by the Czar. All the while, Barnum kept his eyes open the entire trip for new exhibits; he was making money and was anxious to reinvest it in new items for his museum back home. While in London, he tried to buy the birthplace of William Shakespeare, but the deal fell through. Still, he found many smaller items with which to amuse and amaze the folks back home, and by the time he returned, he was the talk of the town and the toast of two continents.

Upon returning to New York, Barnum purchased collections from several other museums to add to his own, including the well-known Peale Museum in Philadelphia. By the end of 1846, Barnum's American Museum was attracting 400,000 visitors a year, and each one paid 25 cents to get in, making Barnum quite a wealthy man. He invested much of his new wealth in a large home for his growing family, as a third daughter, Pauline (born in 1846), now cooed in the nursery.

Called Iranistan, his home featured a unique combination of different elements of Byzantine style architecture, including turrets and onion domes. Referring to its unusual style, Barnum explained:

> "I concluded to adopt it, and engaged a London architect to furnish me a set of drawings after the general plan of the pavilion, differing sufficiently to be adapted to the spot of ground selected for my homestead. On my second return visit to the United States, I brought these drawings with me and engaged a competent architect and builder, giving him instructions to proceed with the work, not 'by the job' but 'by the day,' and to spare neither time nor expense in erecting a

comfortable, convenient, and tasteful residence. The work was thus begun and continued while I was still abroad, and during the time when I was making my tour with General Tom Thumb through the United States and Cuba. Elegant and appropriate furniture was made expressly for every room in the house. I erected expensive water-works to supply the premises. The stables, conservatories and out-buildings were perfect in their kind. There was a profusion of trees set out on the grounds. The whole was built and established literally 'regardless of expense,' for I had no desire even to ascertain the entire cost."

IRANISTAN: THE RESIDENCE OF HON. P. T. BARNUM IN 1848.

Newspaper engraving of Barnum's mansion.

Unfortunately, the $150,000 mansion would stand for only a decade before mysteriously burning down in 1857.

Chapter 3: The Swedish Nightingale

"Jenny Lind: Do you know, Mr. Barnum, that if you had not built Iranistan I should never have come to America for you?

Barnum: Pray explain.

Lind: Well, I had received several applications to visit the United States, but I did not much like the appearance of the applicants, nor did I relish the idea of crossing 3,000 miles of water, so I declined them all. But the first letter which your agent, Mr. Wilton, addressed to me was written upon a sheet headed with a beautiful engraving of Iranistan. It attracted my attention. I said to myself a gentleman who has been so successful in his business as to be able to build and reside in such a palace cannot be a mere adventurer. So I wrote to your agent and consented to an interview, which I should have declined if I had not seen the picture of Iranistan.

Barnum: Then I am fully repaid for building it."

By 1850, Barnum had thoroughly established himself as the premier source of entertainment for the middle and lower classes in New York City, but he continued to be looked down upon by the wealthier, better educated classes, who saw through his humbug and resented what they considered his deceptive practices. With enough money in his pockets to join the upper realms of New York society, Barnum found his way barred by the very nature in which he had made that money, so he began to concoct a plan that would raise the tone of his entertainment, and by extension, he hoped, his reputation.

While he was touring England with General Tom Thumb, Barnum had heard of a singer named Jenny Lind. Originally from Sweden, Lind was at that time the darling of the European aristocracy, nicknamed the "Swedish Nightingale" because of her high, clear soprano voice and her simple, almost shy demeanor. She had a reputation for being devoutly religious and humble in her way of living, and Barnum believed that once she had completed her European tour, she should come and make a concert tour through North America. He offered her an unbelievable deal: he would pay for all her expenses to travel to and through the United States and Canada, as well as give her a salary of $1,000 a concert for 150 concerts. Even as he was brokering the deal, he knew that he was taking a huge chance, telling on friend, "'The public' is a very strange animal, and although a good knowledge of human nature will generally lead a caterer of amusement to hit the people right, they are fickle and ofttimes perverse." Still, he was confident that the American people would be drawn to her and her story of how she planned to donate all the money she made from her tour to the schools located in the poorest parts of Sweden.

Jenny Lind

Having heard of Barnum and his shady business practices, Lind insisted that she get her money up front. He agreed, and she signed the contract, delighted that she would have so much to offer the poor children of her homeland. Now all Barnum had to do was raise the money, and to do this, he mortgaged both his home and his museum. When that did not quite yield enough cash, he met with a well-known minister of a wealthy congregation in Philadelphia. Using all his charms, Barnum explained to the man what an uplifting effect Lind would have on the souls of the American public, if Barnum could just get her to the States. Convinced, the minister loaned him another $5,000.

Part of Barnum's contract with Lind stipulated that she could leave the tour and return to

Sweden after either 60 or 100 concerts, but the she would have to pay Barnum $25,000 if she did. Of course, there was no reason for anyone to be concerned that Barnum would not have plenty of publicity in place prior to arrival. In fact, by the time Lind's ship docked at the New York Harbor on September 1, 1850, the entire nation was in a state of frenzied anticipation that would not be seen again for more than a century. A crowd of more than 40,000 men, women and children were crowded at the dock to meet her ship, with another 20,000 surrounding her hotel when she arrived. The press was everywhere, with every reporter and sketch artist anxious to catch sight of the diminutive singer. Of course, there was also plenty of merchandising, with sheet music and little "Jenny Lind" memorabilia on sale everywhere.

Lind was young and devout, but she was not stupid. When she realized how much money Barnum was making from her appearances, she demanded that they rewrite her contract. Barnum, not willing to take a chance of losing his biggest hit yet, agreed, so on September 3, he signed a new agreement that gave Lind all the profits above the $5,500 guaranteed to Barnum for each concert. Thus, it appeared that one paper may have been right when it published the following:

"I'm a famous Cantatrice, and my name it is Miss Jenny,

And I've come to these United States to turn an honest penny."

The paper then had Barnum supposedly respond:

"We'll welcome you with speeches, with serenades, and rockets,

And you will touch their hearts, and I will tap their pockets;

And if between us the public isn't skinned,

Why my name isn't Barnum nor your name Jenny Lind."

Lind's American tour opened on September 11, 1850 at Castle Garden, and the receipts from that performance alone earned Barnum back more than four times what he had invested thus far. Washington Irving himself praised her performance, writing, "She is enough to counterbalance, of herself, all the evil that the world is threatened with by the great convention of women. So God save Jenny Lind!" His comments and those of others further fed the frenzy, and Barnum began auctioning off tickets for the best seats to the highest bidders. Lind was concerned that the high prices of these tickets meant that fewer people would be able to afford to see her, so she used her charm and clout to persuade Barnum to lower the prices of some of the tickets for each concert to make them more affordable. The press soon forgot the skepticism and began to write instead about the "Lind mania" sweeping the country.

Showman "Walk up Ladies & Gentlemen and see the greatest wonder of the age ... the real Swedish Nightingale the only specimen in the Country"

Newspaper engraving depicting Lind's tour.

To make sure that each community was always in a state of readiness to welcome Lind by the time she got there, Barnum hired 26 reporters to do nothing but write new stories about Lind, her travels and her concerts. After her triumph in New York, Barnum, Lind and their troupe traveled up the east coast into Canada. They then turned south and went down the coast and into Cuba, visiting the Southern states on the way. By this time, Lind had grown weary of Barnum's endless money making schemes, and she took advantage of the clause that allowed her to terminate their contract early. As a businessman, he was satisfied that she had fulfilled her obligation to him and wished her well. Lind finished out the rest of the tour without Barnum, but by that time, he had netted $500,000 from the tour and was well-satisfied with his earnings.

Portrait of Barnum circa 1860, taken by famous photographer Matthew Brady.

"Whatever you do, do it with all your might; work at it, if necessary, early and late, in season and out of season, not leaving a stone unturned, and never deferring for a single hour that which can be done just as well now. The old proverb is full of truth and meaning, 'Whatever is worth doing at all, is worth doing well.' Many a man acquires a fortune by doing his business thoroughly, while his neighbor remains poor for life, because he only half does it. Ambition, energy, industry, perseverance, are indispensable requisites for success in business. Fortune always favors the brave, and never helps a man who does not help himself." – P.T. Barnum

Barnum was determined to use the money he had earned to make his museum and its entertainments "respectable." He was aware that many people still forbade their children from visiting his museum and refused to visit themselves because they felt it was morally corrupt, so he began to focus energy on offering entertainment that he could market as "edifying." Near the Barnum American Museum, he built another large edifice he called the "Moral Lecture Room." He wanted parents and children alike to understand that when they came there, they would see and hear programs that would make them better, happier, healthier people. He then invited some of New York City's most ardent moralists to give speeches there. He was the first producer to ever offer matinee performances at a time when families could attend together without the children getting to bed late. Many people also felt more secure traveling downtown to see a play or hear a speaker when they knew they could be back home before dark.

Barnum's first production in this vein was a melodrama called *The Drunkard*. While it was billed as entertainment, it was actually a thinly veiled lecture on temperance. Barnum had given up drinking alcohol when he returned to America from Europe, so the issue was actually near and dear to his heart. Barnum went on to offer a wide variety of entertainment at the location, from comedic farces to morality tales, and he also brought in well-respected actors to perform plays based on historical events. He even had portions of Shakespeare's plays rewritten for American ears and produced for his audiences.

Mr. Barnum's plan also embraced performances of "moral dramas", such as "Uncle Tom's Cabin," "Moses in Egypt," "The Drunkard," and "Joseph and His Brethren." It is also noteworthy that through these performances, Mr. Barney Williams and Miss Mary Gannon, who subsequently became famous themselves, commenced their careers under his management at very small salaries. E.A. Sothern and many other actors who subsequently became celebrated were also members of the museum's dramatic company from time to time.

Although he was trying to change the nature of his entertainment, Barnum's favorite entertainments remained those that allowed for audience participation and prizes. Each spring and summer brought around flower shows, where his visitors were invited to enter their prize petunias or visionary violets in contests to earn blue ribbons and other prizes. Of course, everyone in the family had to stop by to admire Mother or Uncle Charley's handiwork, and all were welcome so long as they paid 25 cents each. The same was true of the beauty contests, where some lovely young lady would be chosen the fairest of them all, or the dog shows or even the poultry contests. Inevitably, the most popular contests of all were always the baby shows. Every mother in New York knew that her daughter was the prettiest, or that her twins were the cutest, and she just needed Mr. Barnum's fine judges to agree with her. Of course, some contests, such as the fattest baby or the tallest toddler, were more subjective than others.

An 1856 newspaper advertisement for Barnum's museum.

Barnum with Commodore Nutt, another dwarf that performed at his museum.

In 1853, Barnum founded *The Illustrated News*, a paper built around promoting his many projects and selling advertising space. The following year, he completed work on his first book, an autobiography entitled *Life of P. T. Barnum*. While it was popular among great Americans like Mark Twain, European critics panned it, claiming a "sincere pity for the wretched man who compiled it." Still, due to his careful marketing, Barnum's book would go on to sell more copies than any other book in America except the New Testament.

During this time, Barnum began investing heavily in the Jerome Clock Company, one of the major developers of East Bridgeport, Connecticut, but the company went bankrupt in 1856 and suddenly left Barnum penniless. To make matters worse, the following year Barnum's beautiful

Iranistan burned to the ground. As a result of these experiences, he would later write, "Young men starting in life should avoid running into debt. There is scarcely anything that drags a person down like debt. It is a slavish position to get ill, yet we find many a young man, hardly out of his 'teens,' running in debt. He meets a chum and says, "Look at this: I have got trusted for a new suit of clothes." He seems to look upon the clothes as so much given to him; well, it frequently is so, but, if he succeeds in paying and then gets trusted again, he is adopting a habit which will keep him in poverty through life. Debt robs a man of his self-respect, and makes him almost despise himself."

Barnum would spend the next four years rebuilding his wealth and good name. Some, such as Ralph Waldo Emerson, rejoiced in his fall, saying it showed "the gods visible again." However, most people who knew him personally supported his efforts and helped him get back on his feet. Most notably, General Tom Thumb came to his aid; he had been touring for some years independently, but he invited Barnum to stage a European tour for the two of them. Barnum took him up on his offer, and, along with fees for giving temperance lectures, they made enough money to get a new start. He took back his museum and built a new mansion, "Lindencroft," where Iranistan had once stood.

At first, it seemed like Barnum might not be able to recapture the magic of his earlier days, but he was always more interested in the future than he was in the past. He built the first large scale public aquarium in the United States and brought in a white whale to live in it. He also expanded the museum's wax figure gallery and created "Seven Grand Salons," each devoted to one of the Seven Wonders of the World. He enlarged the museum's holdings to include a total of four buildings and even published "Guide Book to the Museum," which was said to include descriptions of 850,000 unusual items.

Barnum got another boost in 1860 when Siamese Twins, Chang and Eng, traveled north from their home in North Carolina to New York. By this time, the two men, who were married to two sisters, had 21 children between them and needed money to send them to college. They agreed to appear at the museum for six weeks, and while they were there, Barnum did amazing business.

Chang and Eng

Though he had once owned Joice Heth, Barnum was politically an abolitionist. He often spoke out against slavery and sectionalism in the days leading up to the Civil War. In 1853, Barnum staged *Uncle Tom's Cabin*, the famous novel written by Harriet Beecher Stowe, but the main distinction in the version played out on stage at Barnum's American Museum is that it had a happy ending, with Tom and the rest of the slaves being freed at the end. When it was well-received by his New York audience, Barnum staged another play based on Stowe's novel *Dred: A Tale of the Great Dismal Swamp*.

In 1854, Barnum split with the Democratic Party over the Kansas-Nebraska Act and joined the newly formed Republican Party. He was an avid supporter of Abraham Lincoln and even arranged for the newly married General Tom Thumb and his equally diminutive bride to visit the White House shortly after their marriage in 1862. By this time, the Civil War was in progress and Barnum was devoting much of his museum space to pro-Union exhibits that encouraged people to stand strong. He also hosted lectures and dramas in support of Lincoln and the war. In 1864, Pauline Cushman, an actress who had spied on behalf of Union forces, visited the hall and gave talks about her adventures.

Unfortunately, not everyone in New York appreciated Barnum's efforts. By this time, the war was becoming increasingly unpopular, and in 1864, an angry arsonist set fire to the museum. It was quickly extinguished, but another fire broke out soon after the war was over and burnt the building to the ground. Spectators were horrified as animals from the museum's in-house zoo jumped from windows to escape the flames, only to be injured and then shot by policemen before they could stampede across the city. Many later recalled that it was the biggest fire they had ever seen in the city. Barnum salvaged what he could and moved it to a new location in the city, but it too burned a few years later. At that point, Barnum decided he'd had enough; he would find a new way to make a living.

Chapter 5: Jumbo

"I had often looked wistfully on Jumbo, but with no hope of ever getting possession of him, as I knew him to be a great favorite of Queen Victoria, whose children and grandchildren are among the tens of thousands of British juveniles whom Jumbo had carried on his back. I did not suppose he would ever be sold." – P.T. Barnum

"Don't disperse your forces. Once occupied with a thing, stick to it until you succeed, or until there is absolutely no hope. By pounding a nail with a hammer, you end up by getting it in, if it can go in. When a man's attention is totally concentrated on a single object, he will find better ways, better procedures which he wouldn't have discovered if he'd been thinking about a dozen different projects, splitting his brain and all his senses. More than once, a fortune has slipped through someone's hands because he undertook too much at the same time. 'Don't hunt two hares simultaneously' says the proverb, and the proverb is right." – P.T. Barnum

While trying to find his new career, Barnum decided to do something for the good of society. In 1865, with many of the nation's leaders either exhausted or dead as a result of the Civil War, there were a number of new openings in government, especially on the state level, so Barnum ran for and was elected to the Connecticut State Legislature to represent his home district of Fairfield. He served two terms in the legislature, where he helped guide the state through the process of ratifying the Thirteenth Amendment, which made slavery illegal in the entire United States. Many people in the North were still not personally opposed to slavery, and those in Connecticut were no different, so Barnum had his work cut out for him. He often made impassioned speeches on behalf of African-Americans in the United States, saying in one speech, "Let the educated free negro feel that he is a man; let him be trained in New England churches, schools and workshops; let him support himself, pay taxes, and cast his vote, like other men, and he will put to everlasting shame the champions of modern democracy, by the overwhelming evidence he will give in his own person of the great Scripture truth, that 'God has made of one blood all the nations of men.'"

Following his success in state government, Barnum ran for the U.S. House of Representatives in 1867 but lost. As often happens in such cases, he swore off politics for a while but eventually got back into politics in 1875, when he successfully ran for mayor of Bridgeport. In this capacity, he led the city in a number of local improvements, including improving the water supply of the city by replacing worn pipes and extending water lines to more outlying regions. He also worked to introduce the first gas lighting for the city's streets, making it safer for people to be out at night and encouraging businesses to stay open later.

Still the crusader, Barnum supported the local liquor laws and fought to make them both stricter and better enforced. He did the same with the laws against prostitution, a problem that was growing increasingly severe as the city itself grew. Concerned about the physical welfare of the town's citizens, Barnum worked with others in the area to found the Bridgeport Hospital in 1878, and when the hospital was incorporated by the state legislature, Barnum served as the first president of the board of directors. He would always maintain, "The foundation of success in life is good health: that is the substratum fortune; it is also the basis of happiness. A person cannot accumulate a fortune very well when he is sick."

Unlike many self-made men of his generation, Barnum claimed not to be interested in sharing his wealth with good causes, at least not in the classic sense. Instead, he embraced what he called "profitable philanthropy" saying, "I have no desire to be considered much of a philanthropist...if by improving and beautifying our city Bridgeport, Connecticut, and adding to the pleasure and prosperity of my neighbors, I can do so at a profit, the incentive to 'good works' will be twice as strong as if it were otherwise." This was obviously true in his construction of his museums and other forms of edifying entertainment, but he also gave quiet donations to other charitable organizations and remembered a number of them in his will. Barnum also donated land in Bridgeport in 1865 for what became the Seaside Park, and what began as 35 acres became 100 acres in 1884. Through the years, the park became a pleasant location for many types of outdoor entertainment that were quite at odds with the kind that could be found in Barnum's museum and circus.

In 1865, Barnum published his second book, entitled *The Humbugs of the World*, in which he sought to make the public aware of just how many ways there were for them to be taken in by unscrupulous con artists. While Barnum himself has been wrongly accused of saying "There's a sucker born every minute," he actually felt very strongly that people should get what they pay for. Following the Civil War, he became involved in many efforts to track down and expose those who would use the public's fear or curiosity to bleed them dry.

One of the causes that Barnum took up was the fight against "spiritual photographs." In the years following the Civil War, the intersection of thousands of grieving family members with advances in the fledgling art of photography created a perfect environment for this new type of con. A photographer would take a photograph of a person and then, when it was developed, a mysterious image of the "ghost" of a lost family member would appear. One of the leaders in this line of work was William Mumler, who ran a thriving New York business by convincing people that if they would have a photograph taken by him, a departed loved one would appear in the background with a message from beyond the grave.

One of Mumler's "spirit photographs" of a woman and her dead brother.

Of course, it took a con to know a con, and as an excellent "humbugger" himself, Barnum knew a hoax when he saw it. He went after Mumler for taking advantage of people in their grief, and when Mumler was finally arrested for fraud, Barnum offered to testify against him at trail. In preparation, he hired a photographer named Abraham Bogardus to take a "spirit photograph" of him with Abraham Lincoln in the background. Then, during his testimony, Barnum showed the photograph to the jury and explained how it was created. Although Mumler was not convicted of fraud, Barnum's explanation made the news and put Mumler out of the spirit photograph business.

In 1869, Barnum published his third book, titled simply *Struggles and Triumphs*. It was something of a sequel to his autobiography and covered his life over the previous four decades. In his preface to the book he observed, "This book is my Recollections of Forty Busy Years. Few men in civil life have had a career more crowded with incident, enterprise, and various intercourse with the world than mine. With the alterations of success and defeat, extensive travel in this and foreign lands; a large acquaintance with the humble and honored; having held the preeminent place among all who have sought to furnish healthy entertainment to the American people, and , therefore, having had opportunities for garnering an ample storehouse of incident and anecdote, while, at the same time, needing a sagacity, energy, foresight and fortitude rarely requited or exhibited in financial affairs, my struggles and experiences (it is not altogether vanity in me to think) cannot be without interest to my fellow countrymen." As always, Barnum knew his audience. Whatever the book might lack in veracity, it more than made up for readability.

Ironically, Barnum was 61 years old by the time he found the calling that he's still most closely associated with. He was visiting some friends in Delavan, Wisconsin when he met William Cameron Coup, and the two men hit it off so quickly that they decided to go into business together. Since Barnum was the famous one, they called their venture the "P. T. Barnum's Grand Traveling Museum, Menagerie, Caravan & Hippodrome", and it was just what it claimed to be: a strange mélange of circus, museum and freak show. As if its first name was not long and descriptive enough, it would later be known as "P.T. Barnum's Travelling World's Fair, Great Roman Hippodrome and Greatest Show On Earth."

Coup

The Only Hippodrome!

COMING IN ALL ITS ROYAL GRANDEUR!

Will Exhibit cor. Michigan Ave., bet. Tenth and Twelfth Sts.,
Detroit, Wednesday and Thursday, Aug. 23 and 24.

W. C. Coup's

New United Monster Shows, Menagerie, Aquarium,

HALL OF STATUES, MUSEUM, AUTOMATIC EXPOSITION,

Three Full Circus Companies and Great World's Fair!

TO WHICH HAS LATELY BEEN ADDED THE

Vast Paris Hippodrome!

——WITH ITS——

COLISEUM AMPHITHEATER!

The Largest Canvas ever made, requiring no less than SEVENTY-FIVE CENTER POLES, all of which are as large as the center poles used in ordinary three and four pole tents, and covering an

Area of Eight Acres!

A RACE TRACK A HALF MILE ROUND AND FORTY FEET WIDE!

3 FULL CIRCUS COMPANIES 3

——IN——

4 FOUR IMMENSE RINGS 4

175 FIRST-CLASS PERFORMERS 175

FRANK MELVILLE and WM. DUCROW, the Champion Riders of the World. M'lle JEANNE, the most Beautiful Woman and the Finest Equestrienne Living. The Celebrated BRONCHOS. The Leaping Horse NETTLE. M'lle ZAOLA, in her Terrific Head-foremost Dive and Eagle Swoop from the Summit of the Amphitheater. LOVAL, the Human Cannon Ball. AK-RE, in her Astounding Leaps. Mme. LOVALE, in her Wonderful Bicycle Act. The Grand Historical Tableaux of the ASSASSINATION OF GARFIELD, and the Identical Clothes which Guiteau wore at the time of the Assassination, and the suit he wore during the trial. Prof. White's Dog Circus and Canine Comedians. Prof. Robert's Brazilian Pony Circus. Trained Elephants. An Immense Marine Aquarium, with its Sea Lions, Sea Leopards, Elephants and Monsters of the Deep. A Grand Free Aerial sight, A BALLOON RACE, unless prevented by storms, will be given every day.

A GORGEOUS OPEN-AIR PARADE!

Will be given between 9 and 10 o'clock. Doors open at 1 and 7 p. m. Performance an hour later. Prices as usual. Children under 9 years, half price. Reserved Seat Tickets can be purchased at a slight advance at PRITTIE'S CENTRAL DRUG STORE.
No camp followers allowed, nor will any gambling or swindling games be permitted on the grounds.

Howell...........................August 23	Evart.........................September 2
Stanton................................ " 26	Manistee............................ " 4
Big Rapids........................... " 28	Ludington........................... " 5
St. Louis.............................. " 29	Cadillac............................. " 6
East Saginaw........................ " 30	Traverse City...................... " 7
Bay City.............................. " 31	Petoskey........................... " 8
Midland..........................Sept. 1	Cheboygan.......................... " 9

An 1882 advertisement of Coup's circus.

After a decade of traveling around on his own, in 1881 Barnum merged with James Anthony Bailey, who was the manager of the "Cooper and Bailey Circus". Barnum had contacted Bailey in part because he was interested in purchasing a young elephant named Columbia that had become part of Bailey's circus, but eventually they moved on to other discussions. By this time, Cooper was no longer in the picture, and Bailey was looking for someone else to team up with, so the two men formed a venture with an even longer name: "P.T. Barnum's Greatest Show On Earth, And The Great London Circus, Sanger's Royal British Menagerie and The Grand International Allied Shows United." Perhaps not surprisingly this cumbersome name was ultimately shortened to simply "Barnum & Bailey's".

Bailey

This new circus was the largest of its kind, exhibiting constant action in three rings instead of the standard one or two. Their most famous act was arguably the most famous in the history of the circus: a giant African elephant named Jumbo. Raised in captivity, the elephant had been a fixture at the London Zoo since 1865, and when Barnum arranged to purchase him in November 1881, many in the city were distraught. Children wrote letters to Queen Victoria asking her not to allow the sale, and musicians wrote songs like "Why Part with Jumbo?" However, Barnum would not be deterred, and after paying $10,000 for the elephant and another $20,000 to bring him across the Atlantic to his new home, Jumbo arrived safely in New York in 1882. The people of London would eventually forgive Barnum, no doubt thanks to the fact he eventually brought his circus to England. Following his death, one paper praised him: "The octogenarian showman was unique. The death of Mr. Barnum removes a noteworthy and almost classical figure, typical of the age of transparent puffing through which the modern democracies are passing. His name is a proverb already, and will continue to be a proverb until mankind has ceased to find pleasure in the comedy of a harmless deceiver and the willingly deceived."

Jumbo in 1882.

In the meantime, Jumbo was first placed on display at Madison Square Garden, drawing enormous crowds of spectators and making back all the money Barnum had spent on him. He remained in New York for the next two years, and in one of his most spectacular stunts, Barnum led Jumbo and 20 other elephants across the Brooklyn Bridge in 1884 to demonstrate that it was safe for pedestrians and carriages to cross.

Barnum also became one of the first circus owners to move his exhibits around the country by train, a major innovation that would allow him to move much larger animals faster than herding them or carrying them in wagons. This also allowed Barnum & Bailey's to go to rural, whistle stop towns where crowds of people would flock to see something so amazing.

Unfortunately, his decision would also lead to an unforeseen tragedy. In 1885, Barnum decided to have Jumbo join his circus, but one summer evening, the elephant was hit by a locomotive in St. Thomas, Ontario and died. Always the showman, Barnum released a dramatic tale to the press about how Jumbo had died trying to save a smaller elephant from being hit, but the truth was not nearly as heroic. The train engine hit and injured the younger elephant first, which was enough to derail the train. Jumbo, who was not on the tracks, was hit directly by the derailed train and killed. After his death, Barnum continued to exhibit portions of Jumbo's body before ultimately donating the skeleton to the American Museum of Natural History in New York. He also had the elephant's skin taxidermied and displayed wherever the circus traveled over the next two years.

Jumbo after being hit by the train.

Barnum in 1885.

It's clear by the steps he took that Barnum insisted the show must go on, and of course it did, with acrobats performing daring acts and the ever popular General Tom Thumb. Following Jumbo's death, he and Bailey parted company, but the two reunited in 1888 with a new project, "Barnum & Bailey Greatest Show On Earth," later renamed the "Barnum & Bailey Circus." This venture was bigger than ever, and in addition to touring America, this circus toured the world. Barnum was determined, as he said, to "impress on the public that we are prepared to keep the show at the top of the heap for generations to come…" He certainly succeeded, as he and his circus became even more popular than ever. In fact, after decades behind the scenes, he finally became part of the act by starring in the show himself, opening the circus with a ride around the arena in a horse drawn chariot. Of all the fans present at any performance, none smiled bigger or laughed louder than Barnum himself. He would later say, "The noblest art is that of making others happy."

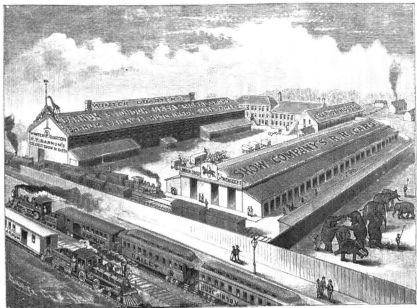

WINTER QUARTERS OF THE GREAT BARNUM-LONDON SHOW.

An engraving depicting the stop in London.

Of course, the majority of Barnum's genius lay in his ability to advertise and stir up interest in what he was selling. He explained his methods in his final book, *The Art of Money-Getting*, which was published in 1880. In this work, he explained the mind behind the man whom some called "The Shakespeare of Advertising." His work has inspired businessmen and executives for decades, especially his saying, "Without promotion something terrible happens... Nothing!" He consistently denied using deceptive practices, instead maintaining that he took what was true and made it more attractive. The bottom line is that he knew people and made his fortune by making people happy.

Chapter 6: Barnum's Final Days

"For the past few years Mr. Barnum's home life was passed quietly at Marina. He was always very happy to see his fellow-townsmen, and to call and chat a few minutes with Mr. Barnum was a pleasure many availed themselves of. Marina, his residence, although small compared to Iranistan and Waldemere, the two mammoth structures he had occupied in this city, is most pleasantly situated at Seaside Park, overlooking the Sound, and is perfect from an architectural point of view. ...he had been a familiar figure on the streets of this city. He always had a pleasant nod for his acquaintances, and oftentimes stopped them to relate some pleasing story." - From Barnum's obituary

Through the years, Barnum made a number of discreet but very large donations to the then new Tufts College in Boston, Massachusetts. He served on the Board of Trustees of the college from the time of its founding in 1854, and for years he gave substantial sums to the school, with the largest being $50,000 donated in 1883 for the construction of the Barnum Museum of Natural History on the campus. Barnum went on to donate most of his vast collection of taxidermied specimens, among them the giant stuffed skin of the famous Jumbo. The circus elephant would go on to become the school's mascot, and the students of Tufts are known even today as the Jumbos. Tragically, fire destroyed the museum and most of the collection in 1975, and rumor has it that the ashes of Jumbo's remains still sit in a 14-ounce Peter Pan Crunchy Peanut Butter jar cared for by the Tufts athletic director. While that's urban legend, it is known that his tail, the only part that survived the fire, is housed in the Tufts Digital Collections and Archives.

Always a man of the people, Barnum championed the cause of holding Sunday afternoon band concerts at Seaside Park "for the benefit of the working people." Many of his wealthy neighbors opposed the plan, afraid that it might attract "the wrong sort" of people to their part of town, and when the first concert was held, the police were called to drive the performers away. According to one account, "Mr. Barnum told the leader of the band to come up to Marina [his home adjacent to the park] and play all day, and the grounds would be free to all who wished to hear the music." In recognition of his generosity, a statue in his honor was raised in Seaside Park in 1893.

In November 1889, Barnum developed a condition that was most likely congestive heart failure. He became too weak to get out of bed and had increasing trouble breathing. He spent most of his time in his room at the beautiful estate, Marina, that he had had built in Bridgeport. Knowing that the end was near, he began to put his affairs in order. He wrote a will arranging for the circus to go on without him under the director of his only grandson, C. Barnum Seeley. He had been grooming Seeley for the business for years and had also recently purchased for him a seat on the New York Stock Exchange. Barnum left the rest of his estate to his wife and two daughters. In a world before the controversy surrounding end of life care, he also left instructions that when the end was near, he be given sufficient doses of sedatives to make his death easier to handle.

Sometime after midnight on April 6, 1890, Barnum suffered a severe stroke. Doctors were called to his bedside, where they found that both his heart rate and breathing had slowed below the point of allowing him to survive. They informed his wife that he would not live much longer, and she called in the rest of the family. Following his instructions, the doctors kept him comfortable to the end, which came just after sunrise on April 7, 1890, but even days before his death, he had insisted that the show must go on, and so it did. According to Barnum's obituary,

"Mr. Bailey said last night that it would have been almost impossible to do anything else. He could not turn away an audience of 10,000 people last night and could not get word out in time to stop hundreds of people coming in from out of town for to-day's performances. He will announce, however, as soon as the day of the funeral is decided upon, that the show will be closed for both performances that day, and all tickets for these performances will either be exchanged or the money therefor refunded."

The obituary went on to say, "Everybody in the company, down to the ring attendants, seemed to be greatly affected at the death of Mr. Barnum and every one had his bit to add to the story of the dead man's kindliness and worth. Mr. Bailey said that his partner's death would make no difference in the show, as by articles of agreement entered into several years ago the company will be held together for many years. The heirs and assigns of both men are directed by the agreement to keep the $3,500,000 capital intact and to continue the present aims and policy of the organization."

The private funeral was held a few days later at the Universalist Church that Barnum had attended. He was then buried at a cemetery he himself had designed, the Mountain Grove Cemetery in Bridgeport. In preparation for his death, he had already had a large headstone put in place at his grave.

When published, his obituary noted that he had left instructions that The Children's Aid Society should receive a portion of each year's circus receipts for as long as the circus remained in operation. In explaining this decision, Barnum told someone, "I don't know anybody connected with that society but I believe in the society. To me there is no picture so beautiful as smiling, bright-eyed, happy children; no music so sweet as their clear and ringing laughter. That I have had power to provide innocent amusement for the little ones, to create such pictures, to evoke such music, is my proudest reflection. I believe this society to be the most practical Christian institution in America. I have catered to four generations of children. I want children to remember me."

While they may not remember his name, most children will always remember their first visit to the circus.

Chapter 7: The Show Goes On

Following Barnum's death, his grandson continued to run the circus, but by 1907, he was tired of being in business and was ready to retire, so he sold the business to the country's other famous ringmasters: the Ringling Brothers. Like Barnum, the Ringling Brothers were another great American success story. There were seven brothers in all and a sister, the children of Marie and August Ringling. Marie and August had been born in Germany and came to the United States along with the first wave of immigrants of the mid-19th century. Their original family name was Ruengling, but like some many others coming to America, they Anglicized their last name to help their assimilation. They initially settled on a farm in McGregor, Iowa, where August farmed during the growing season and worked as a harness maker during the winter, but they eventually moved to Baraboo, Wisconsin.

August and Marie's first son, Albert Charles (Al) was born in 1852. He was joined by Augustus Gustav (Gus), Jr. in 1854 and William Henry Otto in 1858. Three years later, Alfred Theodore (Alf) was born, and then Charles Edward in 1863. John Nicholas arrived in 1866, Henry William George was born in 1868, and their only daughter, Ida Loraina Wilhelmina, was born in 1874. Not surprisingly, a house full of boys came up with many different types of playful and active games, but for the Ringling boys, putting on shows in the backyard would become a way of life. In 1870, when they were still in their teens, Al and Otto created a backyard circus. For a penny, a neighborhood child could see them get a few tame barnyard animals to perform tricks or see something a rare as a bird one of them had trapped in the woods around their home. The older brothers enjoyed entertaining so much that they soon go the younger brothers involved as well. John was particularly adept at entertaining, developing a popular song and dance routine when he was 16 years old.

Alf Ringling

Al Ringling

Charles
Ringling

Otto
Ringling

John
Ringling

The Ringling brothers

On November 27, 1882, Al, Otto, Alf, Charley and John performed an act they called a "Classic and Comic Concert" in the nearby town of Mazomanie, Wisconsin. They enjoyed performing, and their audience liked the show, so they continued to earn money here and there by putting on shows.

In the spring of 1884, they met the famous showman Fayette L. Robinson, known as "Old Yankee." The men hit it off well, and on May 19, 1884, they opened a new show called "Old Yankee Robinson and Ringling Brothers Great Double Show." However, after four years with Robinson, the brothers decided to strike out on their own, subsequently becoming the "Ringling Brothers United Monster Shows, Great Double Circus, Royal European Menagerie, Museum, Caravan, and Congress of Trained Animals." While the Ringling brothers initially got by on their own performances, they soon bought animals to add to the excitement, including an elephant, a trick horse, and a bear. Tickets cost 50 cents for adults and 25 cents for children.

By this time, the brothers had a system of running their business that worked for all of them. As the oldest, Al was the leader, booking shows and deciding where and when they would perform. Otto was the businessman who negotiated the contracts, collected the tickets and counted the money. Alf was in charge of advertising, so he would arrive in town before the others and stir up interest. Charles was the circus manager, making sure that everything looked good and ran smoothly, and finally, John was the head of transportation, ensuring that the horse drawn wagons used to transport the circus operated smoothly. When needed, John also filled in as a clown. Gus never became involved in the circus, choosing instead to remain on the farm with his parents, while Henry, as the youngest, did not join the operation until 1911 after Otto died. He purchased his brother's share of the business and remained with the show until his own death. John would later observe, "We divided the work; but stood together."

In 1889, John followed P.T. Barnum's lead by insisting that the circus trade out their wagons for railroad cars, making theirs one of the first circuses in America to be able to travel across the country. Meanwhile, Otto was busy buying out smaller shows and merging them with theirs, to the extent that he became known as "The King" of circus leaders during the early 1900s. In 1904, he bought a half-interest in the Forepaugh-Sells Circus, which he bought out completely two years later, and in 1907, the Ringling Brothers purchased their only significant competition, the Barnum and Bailey Circus, for $400.000. For the first few years, they treated the two circuses as unique entities, and before long, the brothers needed 100 rail cars to move their circuses from city to city across North America. Of course, they could afford to do this because their earnings went through the roof.

1899 advertisement

A 1900 advertisement for the Ringling Bros. Circus

A picture of the Ringling Bros. Circus, including elephants, train cars, and people, in 1907.

Postcard of the Ringling Bros. headquarters in Bridgeport, CT circa 1911.

In 1905, John married Mable Burton, who hailed from a wealthy New Jersey family that often spent their winters in Sarasota, Florida. Unable to travel during the coldest months of the winter, the circus soon developed the habit of spending the holidays, January and February in southern

Florida as well. The Ringlings' company began buying land on which to live and work during the winter months, purchasing 20 acres of prime waterfront property in 1911.

With no children and plenty of money, the newly married Ringling's also spent much of their year traveling. They made regular visits to Europe, where John checked out new acts for the circus and Mable shopped for art, and through her, John met an import German dealer named Julius Bohler. The three formed a close business relationship, and Bohler helped the wealthy couple purchase some of the finest paintings in Europe, from Rubens to Gainesborough to El Greco. They carefully shipped these pieces home, where many remained in storage until such time as they could be properly displayed.

Tragically, Otto died suddenly in 1911, so Henry took his place as the circus manager. By this time, Al was nearly 50 and was tired of all the traveling associated with circus life, so he began to spend more time at his home in Baraboo, becoming involved in civic affairs there. He built a theater and was recognized by the Wisconsin legislature in 1915 for his contributions to culture in the state, but he died the following year at the age of 61.

By this time, all the brothers were getting up there in years, so they decided to combine the two circuses into one more manageable enterprise. Thus, on March 29, 1919, they opened the Ringling Brothers and Barnum & Bailey Circus at Madison Square Garden in New York City. The posters plasters all over the city announced, "The Ringling Brothers World's Greatest Shows and the Barnum & Bailey Greatest Show on Earth are now combined into one record-breaking giant of all exhibitions!!"

Unfortunately, Alf died that same year, leaving John and Charles to run the circus, but under their management, the circus continued to grow, and it quickly developed a reputation for being one of the most honest, wholesome enterprises of its type in the country. people across the nation not only wanted to attend the circus but join it. One of them was famous photographer Maxwell Coplan (1912-1985), who later published a book about the circus, *Pink Lemonade*, that included historic pictures of it and descriptions of what he saw:

> "When Maxwell Coplan clicks his camera under 'the big top' he gets as great a thrill as the kid who carries water for the elephants. In fact, the circus was responsible for his photographic career. Following his graduation from the Pennsylvania Museum's School of Industrial Art in Philadelphia, where he had been a scholarship student, he was commissioned to do a painting on a circus subject - just one day before the circus was to leave town.

> Working against time, he borrowed a friend's camera and took several pictures of the circus under the friend's direction. He thumbtacked the best one alongside his easel and referred to it for detail. When his client came to see the work, he looked first at the painting, then at the photograph then at Coplan, and said, 'We'll take the

photograph instead of the painting - and we'll pay you the same price!'

Max had spent three weeks on the painting and 1/50th of a second taking the photograph, so he thought he was missing something. He went out and bought a camera identical to his friend's, and before long he was in New York working as a staff photographer on a national magazine. After almost a year in what he considered a rut, spring and the circus came along, and he ran away from his job and joined the circus. Many of the photographs in this book were taken then.

Since then, the camera has taken him around most of the world, on assignments for every national magazine. The work has required him to fly thousands of miles in the past five years, but he still gets a bigger thrill from the man on the flying trapeze - who only flies a few feet!"

Chapter 8: Sarasota

"We bring you the circus — that Pied Piper whose magic tunes lead children of all ages into a tinseled and spun-candied world of reckless beauty and mounting laughter; whirling thrills; of rhythm, excitement and grace; of daring, enflaring and dance; of high-stepping horses and high-flying stars.

But behind all this, the circus is a massive machine whose very life depends on discipline, motion and speed — a mechanized army on wheels that rolls over any obstacle in its path — that meets calamity again and again, but always comes up smiling — a place where disaster and tragedy stalk the Big Top, haunts the back yard, and rides the circus train — where Death is constantly watching for one frayed rope, one weak link, or one trace of fear.

A fierce, primitive fighting force that smashes relentlessly forward against impossible odds: That is the circus — and this is the story of the biggest of the Big Tops — and of the men and women who fight to make it." – Opening remarks from the film *The Greatest Show On Earth!*, a drama set in the Ringling Brothers and Barnum & Bailey Circus.

During the land boom of the early 1920s, Charles Ringling bought up extensive acreage in Sarasota, including purchasing the Gillespie Golf Course and creating the city's first bank, but he died just after his own home on the bay was completed in 1926. He was buried in a large, orange stone mausoleum in Manasota Memorial Park in Sarasota, and his wife Edith remained there, where she continued to help run the circus and stay involved in the community's cultural activities. His daughter, Hester, and her children lived on a comfortable house on the estate, and often participated in local plays and musicals. Reminiscent of the plantations homes of the previous century, the Charles Ringling estate was completely self-sufficient, with its own water supply farm and livestock, and it was run by a staff of servants who lived on the estate. Today, the home Charles and Edith built is part of the New College of Florida campus.

The death of his brother Charles left John on his own. By this time, he was a very wealthy man, having a net worth of around $200 million thanks to wise investments in growing businesses like railroads and oil fields. Like Charles, he had also purchased significant amounts of real estate in and around Sarasota, and he decided to make the area his permanent home. John bought up the small islands along the Gulf of Mexico coast off the edge of the city and made plans to develop them as Ringling Isles Estates. He even built a bridge from the mainland to one of his islands and then donated it to the city. This had the benefit for him of allowing his "snowbirds" access to their new homes over a bridge the city would pay to maintain.

With the remaining brothers moving to Sarasota and spending so much time there, Sarasota eventually became the official winter residence of the circus, and the circus worked with local officials to make the necessary capital investments that would allow the still small town to support the influx of performers. In return, John would arrange for several winter-time performances just for the local citizens.

Meanwhile, John also bought more land for his own use, including bay front acreage formerly owned by Charles Thompson and his wife. There John and Mabel built their dream home, a 30 bedroom mansion designed by the famous New York architect Dwight James Baum. Mable was on hand every day during the house's construction and insisted that only the finest materials be used on every surface. She handpicked everything from the tiles in the bathrooms to the shrubs in the gardens. When it was completed in 1926, they named the Venetian Gothic style mansion, patterned after the style of Mable's much admired Doge's Palace, Cà d'Zan, meaning "The House of John." One writer called it "John's love letter to Mable." It served as the perfect backdrop for the hundreds of art pieces he had purchased during his travels in Europe.

During its heyday in the last roaring years of the 1920s, Cà d'Zan was the center of society and culture in Sarasota. The Ringling's regularly hosted lavish parties that would have rivaled those of the mythical Gatsby of F. Scott Fitzgerald's imagination. Parties in the house and across the spacious lawn would begin as soon as the cruel Florida sun had set, and they would last all night. In order to host the maximum number of guests, John would station the musicians on his yacht, anchored just at the end of the marbled terrace, and people came from all over the country to see and be seen at one of their parties, including the famous Governor Al Smith of New York and the comedian Will Rogers. Flo Ziegfeld would always stop by when in the state, bringing his beautiful wife, actress Billie Burke, with him. Realizing that even their palatial home was not large enough to display all the art they loved, they built a separate museum on their estate in 1927.

John also continued to expand the circus by purchasing the American Circus Corporation in 1929. This umbrella corporation included the Sells-Floto, Hagenbeck-Wallace, John Robinson,

Sparks and Al G. Barnes Circuses, as well as Buffalo Bill's Wild West Show. With that, John Ringling owned a complete monopoly of the circus business in America. Those who traveled to his stately home to meet him might expect a loud, brash showman with a big voice and big personality, but instead, they found a quiet, somewhat shy business man who wore carefully tailored suits and drank his own private-label bourbon. He moved about his palace with the slow pace of someone who was perfectly comfortable surrounded by the finer things in life.

Unfortunately, John reached his peak of success at the worst possible time, because just after he completed this purchase, the stock market crashed and the Great Depression began. While other investors were pulling back, John plunged forward, continuing to buy expensive artwork even while construction on his new projects, such as the Ritz Hotel, remained unfinished. Suddenly, many of his investments were worthless, and almost all his money was gone. To make matters worse, his beloved Mable died in June 1929. She had suffered for years from poorly managed diabetes and the mysterious Addison's disease. Losing his money was one thing, but losing his soul mate was something different entirely. To rebound, he married the young widow Emily Buck of Jersey City, New Jersey a year later.

John was able to retain ownership of his home, museum and art collection, but as a result of the Depression, he lost control of his circus in 1932 when the board of directors, led by his sister-in-law Edith Ringling, chose to incorporate the business and put another man, Samuel Gumpertz, in charge.

John and Emily would get divorced in July 1936, but John died a few months later on December 2, 1936. He was living back in New York City at the time and had contracted pneumonia, but he had remained so determined to recover that he was still looking through catalogues in search of new acts for his "Golden are the Days of Memory" show. When John Ringling died, he had a grand total of $311 in his bank account. Without any children, he left his entire Sarasota estate to the State of Florida, which has managed it and kept it open to the public ever since. His remaining share of the circus went to his nephew, John Ringling North.

Chapter 9: The Greatest Show on Earth

John and Emily would get divorced in July 1936, but John died a few months later on December 2, 1936. He was living back in New York City at the time and had contracted pneumonia, but he had remained so determined to recover that he was still looking through catalogues in search of new acts for his "Golden are the Days of Memory" show. When John Ringling died, he had a grand total of $311 in his bank account. Without any children, he left his entire Sarasota estate to the State of Florida, which has managed it and kept it open to the public ever since. His remaining share of the circus went to his nephew, John Ringling North. North would manage the circus for a few years, cede control over to a cousin, and then take it back a few years later.

Although all the original Ringling brothers were now gone, the circus navigated its way through the Great Depression and World War II to emerge as strong as ever, but there were still issues to deal with. In 1938, the circus tried to bring on Frank Buck, but they had trouble getting around the fact that a union required him to join as an "actor". Buck initially rebuffed the effort, claiming, "Don't get me wrong. I'm with the working man. I worked like a dog once myself. And my heart is with the fellow who works. But I don't want some ... union delegate telling me when to get on and off an elephant." Eventually, everyone got around it by letting Buck avoid being tagged as an actor so long as he merely managed to introduce a giant gorilla for the circus.

John Ringling North and star attraction Frank Buck on an elephant.

Perhaps the most famous incident in the history of the Ringling Bros. and Barnum & Bailey

Circus took place in Hartford in 1944. On July 6, the main tent caught fire, killing over 150 people and injuring hundreds of others among the 7,000 people in attendance. The flames spread as a result of the use of wax to waterproof the tent, making it all the more difficult to extinguish. Survivor Maureen Krekian, who was 11 at the time, described the chaos, "I remember somebody yelling and seeing a big ball of fire near the top of the tent. And this ball of fire just got bigger and bigger and bigger. By that time, everybody was panicking. The exit was blocked with the cages that the animals were brought in and out with. And there was a man taking kids and flinging them up and over that cage to get them out. I was sitting up in the bleachers and jumped down — I was three-quarters of the way up. You jump down and it was all straw underneath. There was a young man, a kid, and he had a pocketknife. And he slit the tent, took my arm and pulled me out." Papers published a photo of clown Emmett Kelly futilely holding a water bucket, and one famous label called it "the day the clowns cried."

Emmett Kelly

Nevertheless, the circus remained one of the biggest entertainment attractions in the country over the next decade, and it was just as giant an operation as ever. Just to come to town, the circus required the use of three different trains, one that consisted of 22 cars for the tents and setup workers, another 28 car train for the canvasmen, ushers and sideshow workers, and another 19 car train that had sleeping cars for performers. Even today, the Ringling Bros. and Barnum & Bailey Circus travels by trains, requiring at least 60 cars that span over a mile.

While the circus is still in operation today and remains popular, the Ringling Bros. and Barnum & Bailey Circus may have been best immortalized in the 1952 film *The Greatest Show on Earth!*. The movie, which won the Best Picture, was a drama revolving around a few characters within the Ringling Bros. and Barnum & Bailey Circus, but in many ways, the circus itself was the star, as the review in *Variety* magazine noted when it said the film "effectively serve[s] the purpose of a framework for all the atmosphere and excitement of the circus on both sides of the big canvas." Shot in Technicolor, the film's visuals impressed audiences and critics alike, and critic Bosley Crowther captured what watching the film was like at the time: "Sprawling across a mammoth canvas, crammed with the real-life acts and thrills, as well as the vast backstage minutiae, that make the circus the glamorous thing it is and glittering in marvelous Technicolor—truly marvelous color, we repeat—this huge motion picture of the big-top is the dandiest ever put upon the screen." A review in *Time* magazine called the film a "mammoth merger of two masters of malarkey for the masses: P. T. Barnum and Cecil B. de Mille...[that] fills the screen with pageants and parades [and] finds a spot for 60-odd circus acts".

Bibliography

Books by P.T. Barnum

Art of Money Getting, or, Golden Rules for Making Money. Originally published 1880. Reprint ed., Bedford, MA: Applewood, 1999.

Struggles and Triumphs, or Forty Years' Recollections of P.T. Barnum. Originally published 1869.

The Life of P.T. Barnum: Written By Himself. Originally published 1855. Reprint ed., Champaign: University of Illinois Press, 2000.

Why I Am A Universalist. Originally published 1890 Reprint Kessinger Pub Co.

Books About P.T. Barnum

Adams, Bluford. *E Pluribus Barnum: The Great Showman and the Making of U.S. Popular Culture*. Minneapolis: University of Minnesota Press, 1997.

Barnum, Patrick Warren. *Barnum Genealogy: 650 Years of Family History*. Boston: Higginson Book Co., 2006.

Cook, James W. *The Arts of Deception: Playing with Fraud in the Age of Barnum*. Cambridge: Harvard University Press, 2001.

Harding, Les. *Elephant Story: Jumbo and P. T. Barnum Under the Big Top*. Jefferson, NC.: McFarland & Co., 2000.

Harris, Neil. *Humbug: The Art of P.T. Barnum*. Chicago: University of Chicago Press, 1973. .

Kunhardt, Philip B., Jr.; Kunhardt, Philip B., III; Kunhardt, Peter W. (1995). *P.T. Barnum:*

America's Greatest Showman. Alfred A. Knopf.

Reiss, Benjamin. *The Showman and the Slave: Race, Death, and Memory in Barnum's America.* Cambridge: Harvard University Press, 2001.

Saxon, Arthur H. *P.T. Barnum: The Legend and the Man.* New York: Columbia University Press, 1995.

Made in the USA
Middletown, DE
09 December 2019